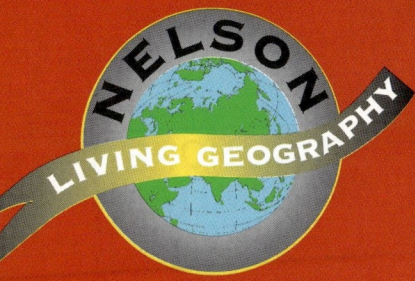

NELSON
LIVING GEOGRAPHY

Living Geography

Book 2

James Dobson

John Sander

Judith Woodfield

Nelson Thornes
Delta Place
27 Bath Road
Cheltenham GL53 7TH
United Kingdom

This edition first published by Nelson Thornes in 2001

ISBN 0-1743-4324-8
01 02 03 04 05 / 10 9 8 7 6 5 4 3 2 1

Printed in Croatia by Zrinski

Typesetting and illustration by Oxford Designers & Illustrators, Oxford

Photo research by Zooid Pictures Limited, London

Acknowledgements

The authors and publisher are grateful for permission to include the following copyright material:

Aerofilms (p. 68); B & D Hosking/Frank Lane Picture Agency (p. 58 top right); BMW (p. 9); Bob Rowan; Progressive Image/Corbis UK Ltd (p. 4 bottom right); Charles O'Rear/Corbis UK Ltd (p. 4 top right); CNES, 1997 Distribution Spot Image/Science Photo Library (p. 72); D T Grewcock/Frank Lane Picture Agency (p. 71 left); Dean Conger/Corbis UK Ltd (p. 94 bottom); Dirk R. Frans/Hutchison Library (p. 94 top); Dylan Garcia/Still Pictures (p. 70); Fred Hoogervorst/Foto Natura/Frank Lane Picture Agency (p. 58 bottom); G.I. Bernard/Oxford Scientific Films (p. 61); Galen Rowell/Corbis UK Ltd (p. 93 bottom); Gordon Hill/Collections (p. 78); Harmut Schwarzbach/Still Pictures (p. 12); Jacqui Hurst/Corbis UK Ltd (p. 40 bottom); Kelvin Aitken/Still Pictures (p. 84); Kim Naylor/Christian Aid/Still Pictures (p. 13); Liz Stares/Collections (p. 46); Map reproduced from Ordnance Survey mapping with the permission of The Controller of Her Majesty's Stationary Office © Crown Copyright; Licence No: 07000U (p. 90); Mark Edwards/Still Pictures (p. 71 right); Michael Busselle/Corbis UK Ltd (p. 69); Nigel Dickinson/Still Pictures (p. 64); Norbert Wu/Still Pictures (p. 83); Owen Franken/Corbis UK Ltd (p. 4 bottom left); Paul Seheult/Eye Ubiquitous (p. 40 top); Photo B.D.V./Corbis UK Ltd (p. 106 top); Purcell Team/Corbis UK Ltd (p. 103); Rex Features (p. 106 bottom); Robert Holmes/Corbis UK Ltd (p. 58 top left); Roger Tidman/Frank Lane Picture Agency (p. 27); Sean Aidan; Eye Ubiquitous/Corbis UK Ltd (p. 4 top left); Sergio Hanquet/Still Pictures (p. 82); Tony Wharton; Frank Lane Picture /Corbis UK Ltd (p. 22); Vauxhall Motors Ltd (p. 6); Wolfgang Kaehler/Corbis UK Ltd (p. 93 top; 104); All others, Judith Woodfield.

Every effort has been made to trace all the copyright holders, but where this has not been possible the publisher will be pleased to make any necessary arrangements at the first opportunity.

Contents

1 Industry

Discussion Points

- Do you think all these people chose the job they are doing? Why?
- Which of these jobs would you like to do? Why?
- Which would you least like to do? Why?

- What would you want a job to give you?
- Sort these jobs into different groups – for example, indoor or outdoor, well-paid or poorly paid.

Types of work

There are many different types of work: paid, unpaid, permanent, temporary, part time, full time, professional, skilled, semi-skilled and unskilled, indoor and outdoor. You can probably think of more types.

The jobs people do are all linked to particular industries. For example, nurses, porters and surgeons work for the health industry, while engineers, designers and salespeople work in the car industry. The word 'industry' is used to describe types of work which produce something or provide a service for other people.

Industry can be divided into three main groups:

Primary industries obtain raw materials from the land or sea. They include farming, fishing, forestry and mining. Sometimes people use the raw material just as it is obtained; for example, when you cook fish or vegetables. Usually the raw materials are *processed* in some way first.

Secondary industries process the raw materials. The fish may be made into fish fingers and the potatoes into oven chips. All *manufactured* goods that you buy have been made by secondary industries, but once they were raw materials. It may take several different secondary industries to make one product; for example, a car factory will put together parts that have come from other factories which produce materials like glass, paint, tyres and cloth.

Tertiary industries do not make any products. Instead they provide a service for people and for other industries. They employ the drivers who deliver the goods and the shop assistants who sell them; they provide you with entertainment, like the music and sports industries; they take you on holiday; they teach you and make you better when you are ill; they repair your broken washing machine and deliver your post.

In many countries there are so many people working in tertiary industries that sometimes this group is split in two. The new group is called the quaternary industries. People working in these industries are still providing a service, but they are essentially involved with high-tech work like research and development and the transfer of information.

Changing industry

A few hundred years ago the majority of people in all parts of the world worked in primary industries. Since then there have been many inventions and developments. Machinery and chemicals mean that more and more food

	UK %	ETHIOPIA %
Primary	2	80
Secondary	27	10
Tertiary	71	10

B Employment in primary, secondary and tertiary industry

and minerals can be produced by just a small number of people, particularly in richer countries. Not all countries can afford to take advantage of these developments, however, and in some parts of the world the majority of people are still working in primary industries. In the world's richest countries, machines are not only taking over jobs in primary industries, but also in factories, and so the number of people working in secondary industries is also going down. More and more people are moving into tertiary and quaternary jobs. Around the world, the leisure and tourism industries are growing fastest.

QUESTIONS

1 Complete this sentence. Choose one of the words primary, secondary, tertiary or quaternary to fill the gap: Leisure and tourism are examples of .... industries.

2 a Look at the jobs in the photographs on page 4. Sort them into lists.
   Draw a table like this:

PRIMARY	SECONDARY	TERTIARY	QUATERNARY

   b Think of some more jobs to add to the table. Write the ones you thought of in a different colour.

3 Why do you think that a few hundred years ago most people in the world had to work in primary industries?

4 Look at table **B**. It shows the types of work done by people in the UK and in Ethiopia. Ethiopia is a country in East Africa.
   a Describe the differences between the type of work done in the UK and in Ethiopia.
   b Why do you think the types of work done in the two countries are so different?

Soils

Nutrients are recycled more slowly during the winter months when decomposers such as fungi and bacteria are not as active. The trees cannot take up as many *nutrients* without leaves. This is because there is no transpiration, and it is transpiration that causes an upward flow of water from the roots. Many of the nutrients stay stored in the soil.

In spring the decomposers break down the leaves on the surface. Earthworms mix up the decomposed leaves with the rest of the soil. There is not as much rain as in tropical rainforests and so not as many nutrients and minerals are washed away.

Trees can be cleared in temperate areas without the devastating effects of tropical rainforest areas but care has to be taken to ensure that soil is not eroded. If roots which hold the soil together are removed, soil can be blown or washed away.

Insects and trees

Temperate deciduous woodlands are not as old as tropical rainforests and contain fewer species of plants and animals. They began to form in Britain after the last ice age, 10,000 years ago. Some of the native species, which have developed naturally in our country, attract more insects than others.

SPECIES OF TREE	NUMBER OF DIFFERENT SPECIES OF INSECTS FOUND ON IT
Oak	284
Willow	266
Birch	229
Hawthorn	149
Alder	90
Elm	82
Ash	41
Lime	31

Non-native trees such as spruce, fir and larch are trees which people have brought into the country. They always have far fewer insect species living on them. Spruce has an average of 37 species, fir 16 and larch 17.

People and trees

Most temperate deciduous forests in Europe and North America have been managed and changed by people. Only Bialoweiza Forest in Poland, which is a World Biosphere Reserve, is thought to be a forest unaffected by the activities of people.

QUESTIONS

1 a Divide a page of your exercise book into four. Draw pictures of the woodland in spring, summer, autumn and winter. Use diagrams **A** and **B** to help you.
  b How have different plants and animals adapted to the temperate climate?

2 a If you were planning a nature area in the grounds of your school and wanted to attract the most insects and birds, which three species of tree would you plant? Give a reason for your answer.
  b Which species would you avoid? Give a reason for your answer.

3 a What is the land in temperate climatic zones used for once it has been cleared of trees?
  b Why is it less damaging to clear temperate deciduous than tropical rainforest?

SUMMARY

- Temperate deciduous forests need at least 350 mm of rain and are found in the temperate climate zone where it is cold in winter but the weather is warm enough for trees to grow for eight months of the year.
- Temperate deciduous forests lose their leaves once a year. The forests have four layers – the canopy, shrub, field and ground layers – and most nutrients are stored in the soil.

FIND OUT MORE ▷ Shaping woods: 68

Shaping woods

FOCUS

- What are woodlands used for?
- What problems can these uses cause?

A

The Forest of Dean, Gloucestershire

Apart from being an important part of the landscape, woods are used by many different people: for breeding game such as pheasants, for sheltering farm animals, for producing timber, for recreation and for wildlife habitats. The Forest of Dean is one of the most important deciduous woods in England. The Dean has produced timber for centuries.

Timber was supplied for weapons in the civil war when hardwood plantations were planted (1642–49). From

Henry VIII's time (1509–47) until the nineteenth century, oak was grown for wooden naval ships. The demand for timber was then met by several conifer plantations which were grown alongside the temperate deciduous trees. All these are now managed by Forest Enterprise.

Forest Enterprise has to try to manage the forest for the needs of timber production, recreation and conservation. Managing forests for all these different things is called multi-purpose management.

B

D The toilet block. Note the gullies on the ground

E The car park

Managing for tourism and recreation

The Forest of Dean is also extremely important for tourism and recreation. The scenery is an important attraction but there are also water sports, walking, cycling and climbing.

Large numbers of tourists could disturb much of the wildlife in the woodlands. In summer this is not such a problem because the trees give a lot of cover and birds and animals can hide easily. However, traffic noise has been proved to affect the breeding success of some song birds. It is believed that in spring the birds cannot hear the mating calls due to the noise and therefore do not breed next to main roads. There are also some rare peregrine falcons in the forest.

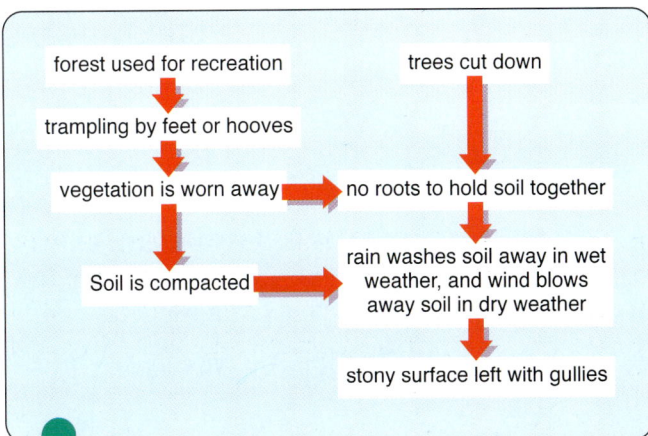

forest used for recreation → trampling by feet or hooves → vegetation is worn away → no roots to hold soil together

Soil is compacted → rain washes soil away in wet weather, and wind blows away soil in dry weather

trees cut down → no roots to hold soil together → rain washes soil away in wet weather, and wind blows away soil in dry weather → stony surface left with gullies

C The causes of soil erosion

QUESTIONS

1 Trace photo **A** of the Forest of Dean and shade the following areas in different colours: temperate deciduous woodland, coniferous woodland, areas for footpaths.

2 Describe the attractions of the Forest of Dean for tourists.

3 One of the biggest pressures on the forest is tourism.
   a Look at photographs **D** and **E**. How have Forest Enterprise tried to manage some of these pressures?
   b Suggest what else Forest Enterprise could do to manage the pressures

SUMMARY

- Woods are used for game, wildlife, timber, recreation, grazing and shelter.
- Grazing can cause problems with woodland regeneration. Tourism can cause soil erosion and disturbance to wildlife.
- Over-use of the forest can also lead to soil erosion (see diagram C).

FIND OUT MORE ▷ Deciduous forest: 66 ▷ Boreal forest: 70

Boreal forests

FOCUS

- Where are boreal forests found?
- What are boreal trees like?
- What problems does the boreal forest face?

Developing boreal forests

Boreal forest replaces deciduous forest as the dominant vegetation when the growing season is below six months and there are fewer than four months with no frost. Most of the trees are conifers, which means that they usually have needle-like leaves and their seeds are found in cones.

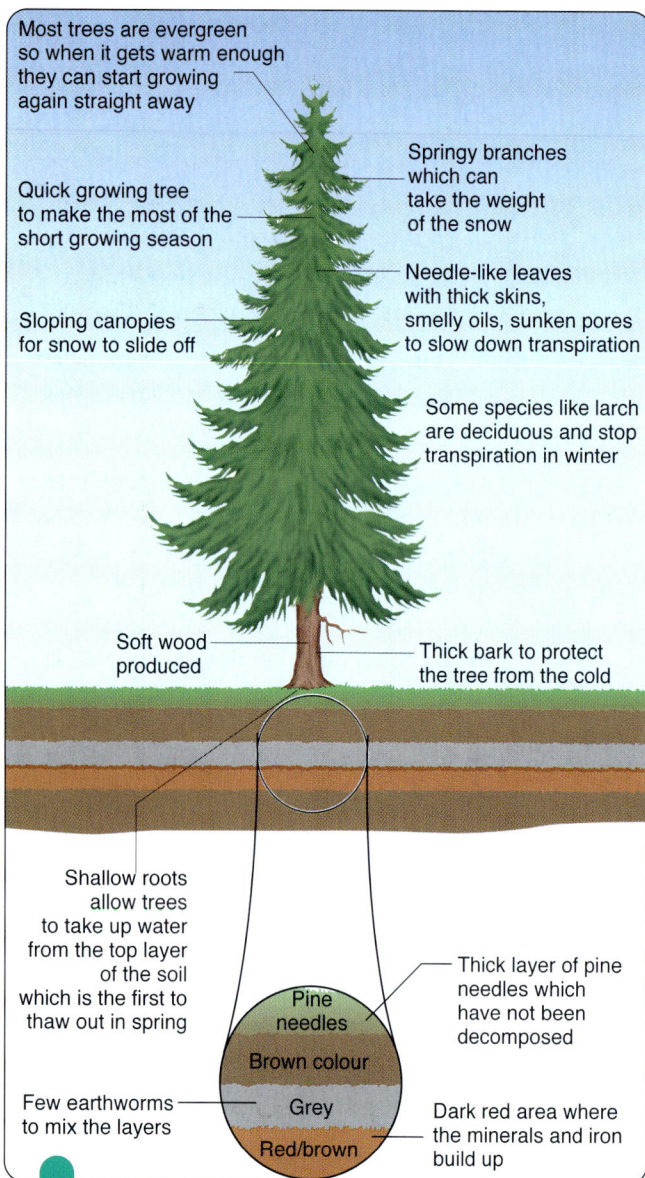

The low temperatures mean that fewer decomposers live in these forests. Earthworms do not like the acid soil and so layers are not mixed in the soil.

In the British Isles the Highlands of Scotland fall into the Boreal zone (map **B** page 59). Here the native trees are Scots pine. Only 25 per cent of the Scots pines which were growing in 1957 were still found in 1990 because so many were cut down and re-planted with non-native conifers such as larch. The remaining pine forest is now found only in nature reserves, unfarmed steep-sided valleys, areas with few sheep, and areas where grants have been used to replace non-native trees. Native pine forest contains some very rare and interesting wildlife like the capercaillie, a large bird.

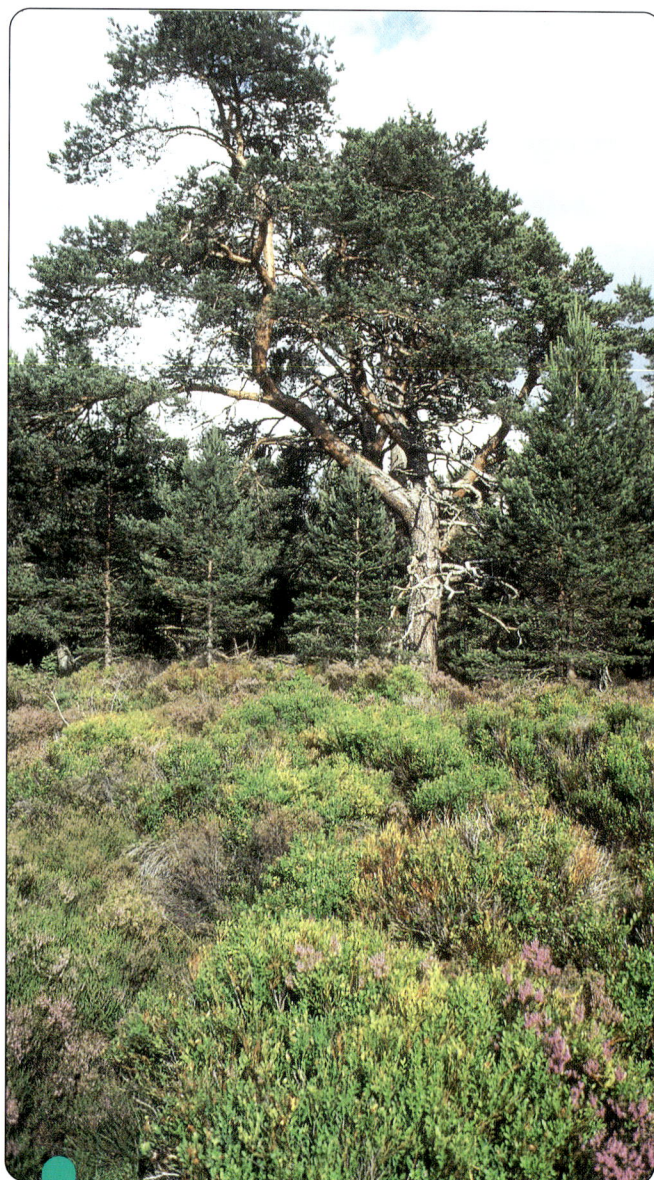

Most trees are evergreen so when it gets warm enough they can start growing again straight away

Quick growing tree to make the most of the short growing season

Sloping canopies for snow to slide off

Springy branches which can take the weight of the snow

Needle-like leaves with thick skins, smelly oils, sunken pores to slow down transpiration

Some species like larch are deciduous and stop transpiration in winter

Soft wood produced

Thick bark to protect the tree from the cold

Shallow roots allow trees to take up water from the top layer of the soil which is the first to thaw out in spring

Thick layer of pine needles which have not been decomposed

Pine needles

Brown colour

Grey

Red/brown

Few earthworms to mix the layers

Dark red area where the minerals and iron build up

A Adaptions of boreal trees

B Scots pine forest

C Plantation forest

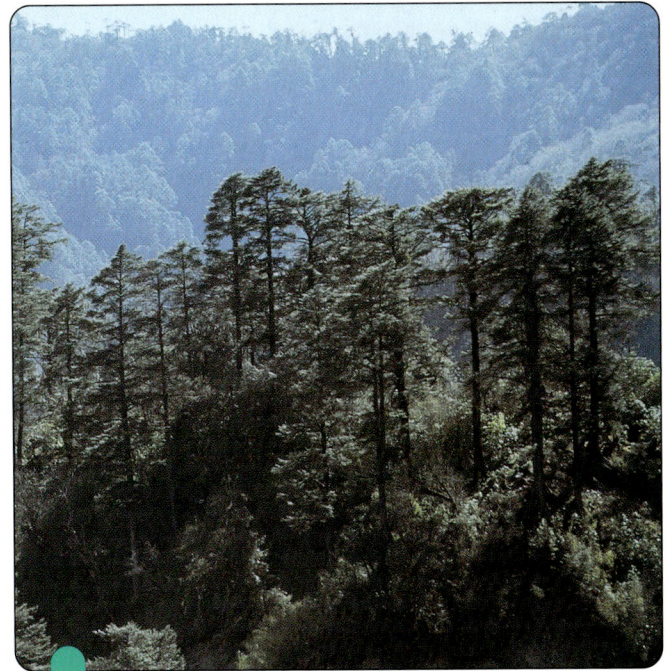

D Natural forest

Planting non-native conifers

Soft wood conifers can grow very quickly. A Douglas fir tree will reach full size in 60 years, whereas an oak will take 100 years. Non-native conifers have therefore been planted outside the Boreal zone for quick timber production. In 1984 the UK Forestry Commission reached a target of 2 million hectares of woodland used for timber. Most of this has been planted in upland areas.

QUESTIONS

1 a Fill in the gaps, choosing from the words listed:
      hard, soft, slow, fast, few, many, light, dark.
      Boreal trees grow .... They produce
      .... wood and have .... insects living
      on them. They grow close together making the
      forest ...., which stops plants growing
      beneath them.
   b Use the words you did not choose to write about
      temperate deciduous woodlands.

2 Why would a native Scots pine forest not be as
   good for producing timber as a non-native
   plantation?

3 a Why might a conservationist prefer temperate
      deciduous trees in lowland areas to non-native
      conifers?
   b Why might a landowner prefer to plant conifers
      on his/her land?

Some 50 per cent was in Scotland where 12 per cent of the land is afforested. Afforestation is the planting of trees where none have been grown before.

Conservationists who look after wildlife are not happy about these changes to the landscape. This is because a lot of the land that has been planted was once very important heather moorland, which is a very rare habitat.

However, in the UK forestry is still a large rural employer with six more jobs per hectare than farming. This is why forests have also been planted in lowland areas.

The plantations are dark and not many plants grow under them. There are few insects, birds and mammals that live in them. Sometimes the soils change underneath and become more acid which means fewer earthworms. Drainage ditches which are dug out close to conifer plantations can speed up the time it takes for water to run off the land, causing floods.

SUMMARY

- Boreal forest is found where the growing season is less than six months.
- Boreal trees have adaptations to lower temperatures, which include very rapid growth that makes them useful for timber.
- In areas away from their natural habitat the boreal species can change soils and landscapes and other ecosystems.

FIND OUT MORE ▶ Shaping woods: 68

Extensions

1 The following fieldwork results were collected in the Forest of Dean by Year 8 students looking at the differences between deciduous and coniferous woodland planted in a lowland area.
  a Describe what the data show.
  b Explain the differences between the coniferous area and the deciduous area.

MEASUREMENT	DECIDUOUS	CONIFEROUS
pH (How acid the soil is) (1=acid, 7=neutral, 8+=alkaline)	5.7	5
Leaf litter (depth in cm) (This is the layer of leaves which have fallen from the trees onto the ground)	1 cm	5 cm
Amount of mini-beasts (High, medium, low)	High/medium	Low
Soil texture (Silty soils are the best for growing crops. Clay is very sticky and sand lets water through easily)	Silty clay	Sand silt
Soil moisture (1=dry, 10=wet)	7	3
Light at ground. Scale (0=dark, 10=very bright)	4	0.5
Light at 2 metres. Scale (0=dark, 10=very bright)	6	0.5
Plant cover on ground per metre square (High, medium, low)	High	Low
How much top layer of the forest is covered by leaves	50%	100%

2 Describe the differences between these three leaves. Explain how they are adapted for the climate they are found in.

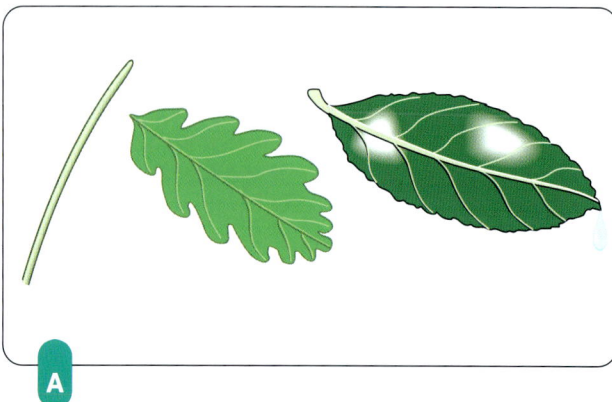

3 a Describe what is happening in this satellite picture of Indonesia.
  b Why is the burning of the rainforests a problem for everyone in the world?

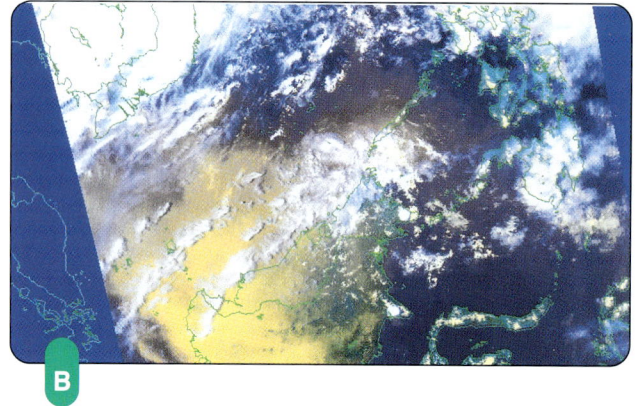

4 a Draw this table and fill in the missing information to describe the differences between these three types of forest.

	TROPICAL RAINFOREST	TEMPERATE DECIDUOUS FOREST	BOREAL CONIFEROUS FOREST
Soil			
Plants			
Animals			
Insects			
Type of wood			

  b What is the main influence on all these forests?
  c Which forest do you think is the hardest to manage? Give reasons for your answer.
  d Which type of forest is most threatened? Give reasons for your answer.

5 a If you were a conservationist, where would you go to study the following:
  • Bluebells?
  • Orang-utans?
  • A temperate deciduous forest which has not been changed by people?
  • Scots pine trees?
  • Termites?
  b Explain why each of these living things is special.
  c Describe how each of these living things could be looked after.

6 Why are native Scots pine trees not often found where there are a lot of sheep grazing?

Glossary

Adapted/Adaptation: Any characteristic that helps plants and animals survive in a particular environment.

Afforestation: The large-scale planting of trees in an area which was not forested before.

Biomes: Global-scale ecosystems.

Canopy: The tops of one or more trees.

Chlorophyll: The green colour in moist leaves which helps them to trap the sun's energy.

Conifers: Cone-bearing trees with needle-like leaves.

Decomposition: Breaking down of dead animals and plants by fungi and bacteria.

Dominant species: This is the species in an ecosystem which will be the largest in number.

Ecosystem: A group of living things which live together in an environment.

El Niño: An ocean current which changes the climate around the Pacific Ocean.

Environment: All the things that affect an ecosystem. These can be living, such as other animals and plants, or non-living, such as soil, climate and rocks.

Environmental Impact Assessment: When people want to develop an area in any way, it is a good idea to complete an EIA which will consider the good and bad points of the development.

Forest Enterprise: Forest Enterprise is responsible for the multi-purpose management of the Forestry Commission's own woodlands and forests.

Management (including multi-purpose management): Using resources for a particular purpose, such as recreation, conservation and landscape value. Where the resources are managed for more than one purpose this is known as multi-purpose management.

IMF: The International Monetary Fund gives loans to countries from the world's central banks.

Minerals: These are chemicals formed from the breakdown of rocks.

Native: These are plants and animals which have arrived in a country naturally without the help of people.

Nutrients: Chemicals needed for living, growing and breeding.

SSSI: Site of Special Scientific Interest. Areas with the best examples of British wildlife, geology and landforms. SSSIs are protected by a series of management agreements with the owners of the land.

Sustainable: The development of a resource or an area so that it remains undamaged for future generations.

Transmigration: Planned movement of people from one area of a country to another.

Transpiration: The loss of water from a plant by evaporation.

Weathering: This is the breaking up of rocks by weather, plants and animals.

World Biosphere Reserve: These were selected by UNESCO as reserves which represent the natural areas of the world. Each reserve has protection for the future and is large enough for effective conservation and for different uses to be allowed without conflict.

A Dunster

B Dunster

C Dunster

D Dunster

E Exe Head

F Farmland

G Lynmouth

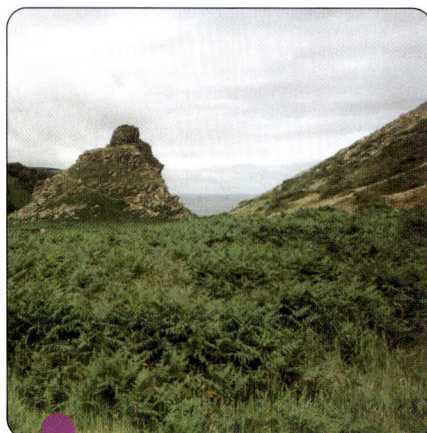

H Valley of the Rocks

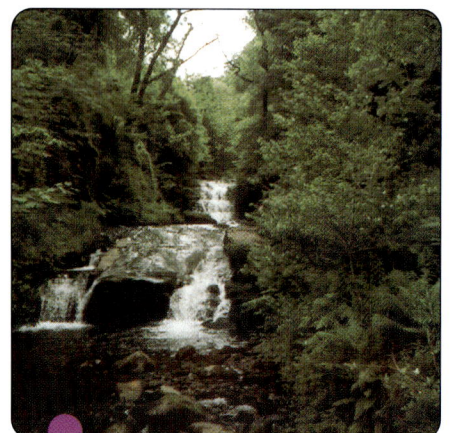

I Waters Meet

Discussion Points

These are all photos of Exmoor National Park, which covers parts of Somerset and North Devon.

- Which landscape do you like best? What could you do if you visited Exmoor National Park?
- How do you think people earn their living in Exmoor National Park?

- What sort of problems might occur for people who live and work in a National Park like Exmoor?
- What sort of problems might occur when tourists come to the National Park?

ADJECTIVE (FEELINGS)	1 (VERY)	2 (QUITE)	3 (NEITHER ONE THING OR THE OTHER)	4 (QUITE)	5 (VERY)	ADJECTIVE (FEELINGS)
Dirty	1	2	3	4	5	Clean
Ugly	1	2	3	4	5	Beautiful
Boring	1	2	3	4	5	Interesting
Noisy	1	2	3	4	5	Quiet
Poor smell	1	2	3	4	5	Good smell
TOTAL						

J Attitude assessment

HOW MANY?	NONE	A FEW	SOME	MANY	A LOT
Flowers and other small plants	1	2	3	4	5
Different kinds of trees	1	2	3	4	5
Birds or signs of birds	1	2	3	4	5
Signs of other animals, creatures such as insects, snails	1	2	3	4	5
Interesting features such as ponds and streams	1	2	3	4	5
Interesting views of the landscape	1	2	3	4	5
TOTAL					

K Factual assessment

What is a National Park?

Some of the most beautiful areas of England and Wales have been made into National Parks. Exmoor has been a National Park since 1954. It covers 693 km² of upland in Devon and Somerset and has many isolated villages.

National Park Authorities help to look after National Parks by having planning rules for the people who live and work there. They make sure that people are able to earn a living and have good facilities in their villages. However, like all other National Parks, Exmoor aims to keep its special landscape, wildlife and historical interest safe for future generations.

A beautiful view!

Often the beauty of a place is judged differently by different people. We can try and measure this beauty by completing an attitude assessment. The results of this assessment measure your emotions and how you feel about a place. Beautiful places are not the only important environments, however, and sometimes landscapes which look ugly may be important for wildlife. We should therefore also look for particular features which will tell us of its wildlife or landscape importance. Feelings and facts together can give us clues about the importance of a place.

If many people survey the same places, we can find average scores which will identify the most popular places overall. To complete an attitude assessment, choose one of the pictures on page 74. Look at it carefully. Now look at Table J. Start with the first pair of adjectives. Decide whether the place in the photograph is very dirty (1), very clean (5) or somewhere in between. Continue down the list. When you have made your choices, add up the total score. To complete the factual assessment look for evidence of each natural feature. Decide whether there is no evidence, a lot or somewhere in between. Add up the total score for this assessment too.

QUESTIONS

1 a Use the attitude and factual assessment charts to score each of the photographs on page 74.
  b Which photograph scores highest in your attitude assessment?
  c Which photograph scores highest in your factual assessment?
  d What do high scores tell you about a place?
  e Collect scores for the rest of your class and find the averages for each photograph.
  f Compare results with the rest of your class.

FIND OUT MORE ▷ Tourism in the UK: 16

Red light for Dunster

FOCUS

- How does traffic affect villages in Exmoor National Park?
- How can traffic problems be reduced?

Managing traffic in villages

Living in the countryside can mean being a long way from the nearest services. Good transport is essential. Eighty three per cent of people living in Exmoor villages own a car. However, 80 per cent of local people are worried about traffic problems. Many residents have to park on the streets because their houses were built before there were cars and garages. Local people often get annoyed when their parking space is taken by a tourist visiting the village. The villages most affected in this way are Dunster, Porlock, Dulverton and Lynton/Lynmouth. These are all honeypot sites for tourists. Honeypot sites are the places that have the attractions that most people want to visit.

The problem is that providing more car parks or improving the narrow roads would only encourage more cars and cause more damage. The National Park Authority has decided that it should not build lots of new car parks to cope with the busiest times. This would be unsustainable and damage the environment, as it would use up more land and encourage too many tourists. Making the area difficult to park in actually helps keep a manageable balance of visitors.

People building new houses must follow strict rules issued by the National Park Authority to stop parking problems. Each new house or flat must have two parking spaces, guest houses must have one per bedroom, and restaurants and bars must have one for every four seats.

The National Park Authority is trying to improve public transport and reduce the use of the car. They encourage tourists to use buses during their stay. One way is to use park and ride schemes, where people park their car a distance away from an attraction and then catch a bus to reach it.

Traffic management in Dunster

Dunster is the jewel in the crown of Exmoor villages. It has 120 listed buildings. Many survive unchanged since the sixteenth century and the basic street patterns still exists. The village has an unusually high number of services. This is not just to serve its population of 848

A A coach coming into Dunster High Street (991438)

people, but also to serve the tourists who visit here all the year round. The village has approximately 5,000 cars visiting daily in August. It has 156 car parking spaces on streets and a further 418 spaces in its two main car parks. You can find the car parks at 993439 and 992436 on map **B**.

Dunster is a conservation area and local people are annoyed by tourists parking along the streets, causing traffic congestion and destroying the historic buildings by pollution and traffic vibrations. In the High Street (991437), West Street (989434) and Park Street (989433) parked cars affect the visual quality of the street scene and cause problems with through traffic. The Park Authority wants to remove the through traffic and reduce the on-street parking. Pedestrians will have priority, providing a much better environment for visitors and residents. However, local businesses are extremely worried that if all these schemes prevent cars driving through the village, fewer people will stop to buy goods.

Some options which might solve the traffic problems

- Build a bypass through Dunster Deer Park or through a tunnel in Grabbist Hill (987434). These would both have huge environmental impacts. There may be more problems than advantages and there is not enough money for this now.
- Less on-street car parking will be allowed on the High Street.
- The car park in Park Street (989432) and on-street car parking will be for residents only.
- A park and ride scheme for the village will provide enough spaces for all the visitors. Visitors will be able to walk to Dunster or catch a bus from a car park off the A road.
- Bus services will be improved so that more services are provided and the buses will be well advertised in local towns like Minehead.

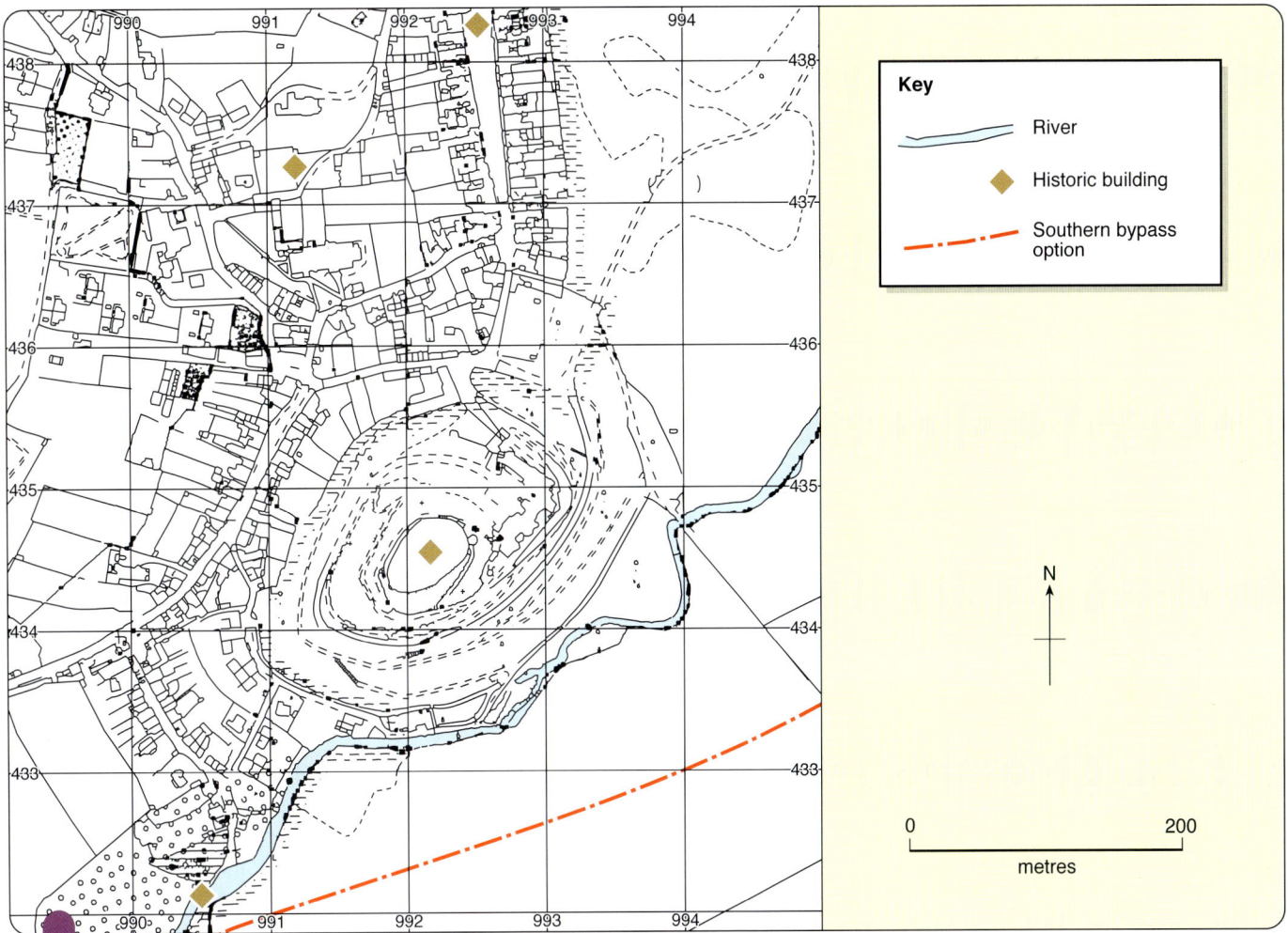

B Dunster and transport ideas

QUESTIONS

1 What was the result of your environmental assessment on page 74 for photograph **A** of Dunster High Street? Do you think that cars spoil the look of the street?

2 a Measure the width of the High Street in square 991437 and Church Street in square 990436. Use the scale to work out their widths in metres.

b An average family car is 1.5 metres wide and drives one metre away from a footpath which is one metre wide. What would be the distance between two cars passing each other in Church Street and in the High Street?

c What types of vehicles would cause further problems?

d Why do people park in the High Street? Think of several reasons.

3 Look at photograph **A** and map **B** and also photographs **A**, **B**, **C** and **D** on page 74. Photograph **B** shows Park Street. Photograph **C** shows the River Avill next to the bypass site and photograph **D** shows the route of the proposed bypass through Dunster Deer Park.

a What would you do to manage traffic in Dunster? You can choose from the list of options on page 76 or make up your own plan.

b Give reasons for your decision.

SUMMARY

- Exmoor honeypots suffer from too many tourists in summer. There is often on-street parking and congestion causing problems for locals.
- Problems can be reduced by making traffic schemes more sustainable. This may mean more public transport, less parking space or fewer parking zones.

FIND OUT MORE ▷ A marina plan for Watchet: 56–57

Living Exmoor style

FOCUS

- What do buildings on Exmoor look like?
- How does the National Park Authority protect the character of built-up areas?

Exmoor buildings

Many different types of building can be found across Exmoor. The differences depend on things like the age of the settlement and the type of building materials available. Settlements inland, like Dunster and Allerford, often grew from farming communities and have some very old buildings. Many of the settlements on the coast grew rapidly during the nineteenth century and so have newer buildings. Lynton has Victorian architecture as well as evergreen vegetation.

Allerford has cottages built of stone and thatch such as those shown in photograph **B** on page 74. Buildings in Dunster are mainly of red sandstone. On the moors where there is more rain and wind, farms have been built in hollows, sheltered from the wind.

Keeping the traditional style

The National Park Authority takes great care to keep traditional architecture throughout Exmoor. They therefore give advice on acceptable building types. Planning applications which do not fit in with the landscape will be rejected. Some of the advice they give is shown in diagrams **B** and **C**.

Roof materials were either very thick, heavy stone tiles or thatch.

Roofs were covered in roof tiles and were very steep.

If buildings were built in a more exposed place, then shelterbelts of trees were planted around them.

Sometimes the rubble walls were limewashed, white or cream.

Since the nineteenth century, thatch has been replaced by natural slate, particularly in areas of heavier rainfall.

The farmhouses have very thick walls, big chimneys and low, deep porches to protect the doors.

Buildings were built around yards for protection, with blank walls on the outside.

Windows were small.

A An Exmoor farm

Don't

flat roofed dormer

flat roof extension

old cottage

non-native tree species

timber fence panels

glass door

detached garage

large window

many different materials which are very muddled

standing space for a car

concrete block decorative screen walling

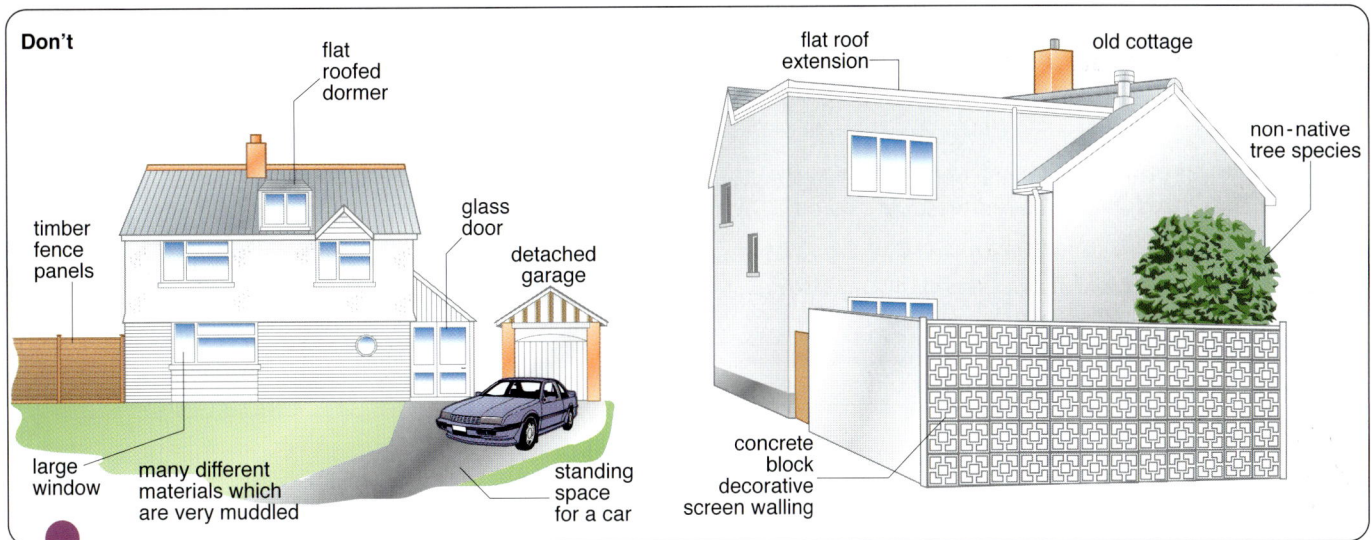

B Unacceptable house design on Exmoor

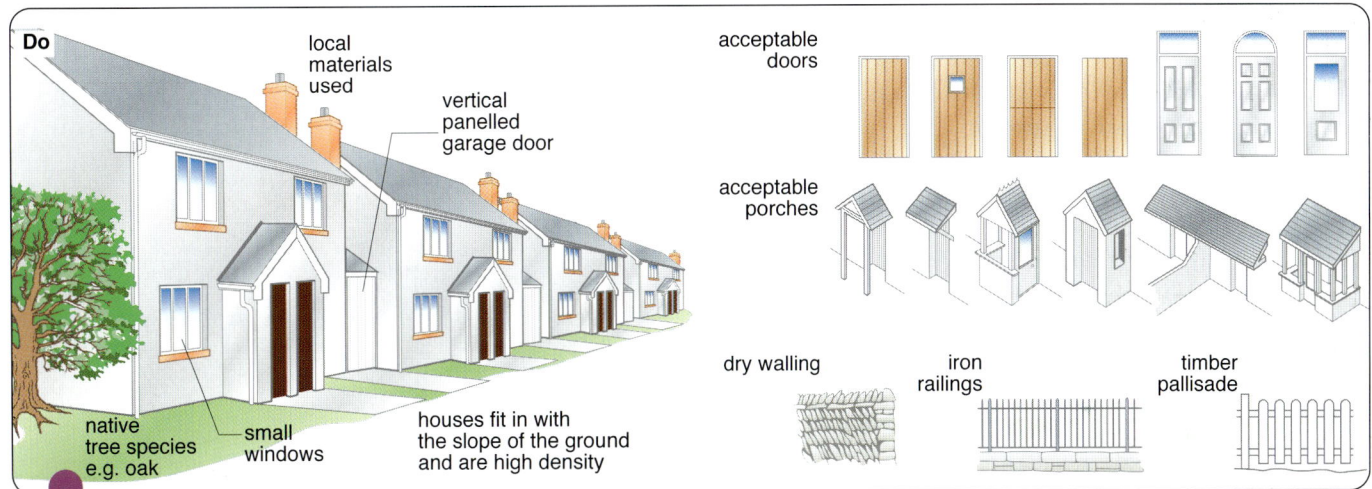

Do

local materials used

vertical panelled garage door

acceptable doors

acceptable porches

native tree species e.g. oak

small windows

houses fit in with the slope of the ground and are high density

dry walling

iron railings

timber pallisade

C Acceptable house design on Exmoor

QUESTIONS

1 Look at diagram **A**. Why do you think the house has:
a thick walls? b small windows?

2 Why do you think the National Park Authority takes such trouble to make sure the buildings are designed in a certain way?

3 You have planning permission to build a two-bedroomed cottage on the land behind the fence in photograph **D** page 74. This is in square 989432 on map **B** on page 77. The land is reached along Park Street (photograph **B** on page 74) and faces the cottage shown in photograph **C** on page 74.

a Use these and other photographs of Dunster and diagrams **B** and **C** to help you design a cottage for this area of land.

b Label the drawing to explain how it will meet all the planning rules.

SUMMARY

• The appearance of buildings on Exmoor varies according to the date they were built and their location. No one style dominates.

• The National Park Authority gives guidelines to help people with the planning of new houses or the renovation or conversion of older ones.

FIND OUT MORE ▷ Your environment: 86

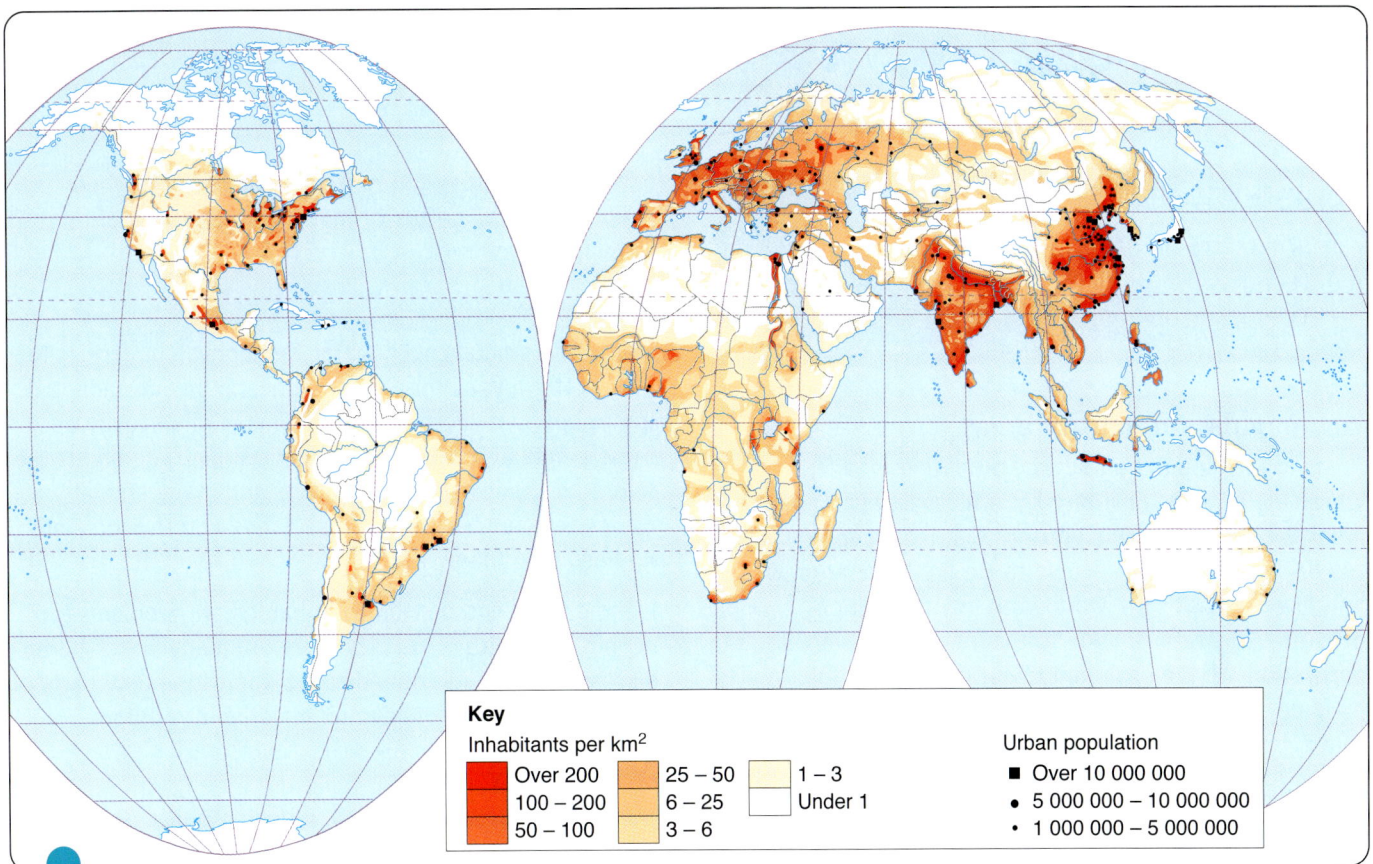

C Population density and distribution

Key

Inhabitants per km²

■	Over 200	■	25 – 50	□	1 – 3
	100 – 200		6 – 25		Under 1
	50 – 100		3 – 6		

Urban population

■ Over 10 000 000
● 5 000 000 – 10 000 000
· 1 000 000 – 5 000 000

What is population density?

Population density is the average number of people per km² of land. For a country as a whole the figure can be as low as 0.04 per km², which is the density in Western Sahara in Africa, or as high as 577 per km² for Singapore in Asia. As this is an average figure for the whole country, it means that there may be some areas within the country which are more densely populated and have many people per km², and others which are sparsely populated and have few people per km².

What is population distribution?

Population distribution is where people are found. People may be concentrated in a few places or scattered over a wide area.

Areas of high density can be found along river valleys, coasts and close to important resources such as mineral deposits. Very often these are places where in the past many people survived due to good food supplies or were able to trade other products for food. Huge cities have built up in these places. The conditions in these cities vary. An area of very high population density such as Singapore may have more people, but good building design and a wealthy population mean that the standard of living is good. In other areas high densities can put pressure on resources and there may be overcrowded buildings and poverty. High densities of population are therefore much easier to manage in richer countries.

In 1999 the world's population reached 6 billion. If the whole world was as densely populated as Singapore, there would be space for 550 billion people. However, 80 per cent of the world's population lives in only 20 per cent of the area. This means that some places have low densities and there are several reasons for this.

Living on the edge

FOCUS

- Where are areas of low population density found?
- Why do people not live in these areas?

Low population density areas

Areas of low population density are found in places where the physical environment affects survival. Some areas are too hot, others are too cold, too steep, too wet, too dry or too high for people to live in. There are fewer and fewer areas in the world with low population densities. This is partly due to the increase in the world's population. People have had to cut down more forest, build on steeper land and drain wet land to provide living space. Technological advances such as central heating, refrigeration and improved transport mean that people can now live in environments which were not suitable before. They are also able to use resources that were previously inaccessible.

Altitude

Temperature decreases by about 6.5°C for every 1,000 metres and so the very highest areas of the world are always covered by snow and ice. They can also be swept by very strong winds. Most plants need a temperature of about 6°C to grow and therefore only a few species of plants can grow when temperatures are lower than this. Higher altitudes also result in some health problems for humans new to the area. People have to acclimatise gradually as they climb up a very high mountain, otherwise they run the risk of a condition called altitude sickness. Slopes are often too steep for farming.

Latitude

Places which are within 20 degrees latitude of the north and south poles are likely to be very cold. Areas in the Arctic and Antarctic may go without sunlight for several months of the year, which limits the growth of plants. Up to six months of darkness and temperatures below -20°C make life difficult.

Between the tropics the sun's rays are intense and plant growth is rapid. However, the nutrients are stored in the thin top layer of the soil and in the plants. When people cut down the forests for farmland, they can not stay on that patch of land long before the heavy rains wash away all the nutrients. People have therefore found it difficult to live at high densities in some Equatorial areas. The rainforest is best suited to a nomadic lifestyle where people hunt and gather or move from one area of farmland to another.

Water

Plants and animals need water for survival. In deserts too little water means that only plants and animals adapted to drought can overcome this. Humans rely heavily on these plants and animals for their survival. The plants are scattered thinly across the deserts and many animals wander in search of food. Most native desert people are nomads who follow them.

If the ground is too swampy, it can create problems for people. In tropical countries there are many water-borne diseases such as river blindness. Swamps in many parts of the world may also encourage malarial mosquitoes.

Accessibility

Tropical rainforests and steep, rugged mountains discourage people from living in some areas. Developing industry in such areas is difficult and expensive. Many of these areas, which were originally not lived in because they are out of reach, are now wildlife reserves or National Parks. Wildlife has survived in these places because people have not had the chance to disturb them.

Where people are found is not just due to the physical environment. Population density is also linked to population growth and development. People live at the hub of the population wheel (diagram **A**) and are affected by all the reasons shown around it. Many of these issues will be looked at within this unit.

Population wheel

To understand how the wheel works, go to its centre. This is where all the world's people are. Here the people causes change and are affected by change themselves. The number of people at the centre, how quickly they give birth and what their lives are like, is linked to all of the spokes which join the rim. The environment, economy, politics and social conditions all affect people at the centre. However, these people all affect the spokes. As the wheel moves forward, time moves on and the balance between the items on the spokes change. For example, the war in Sierra Leone in West Africa meant that politics had strongest effect on the people in 2000. A flood in Bangladesh in 2000 meant that the environment had the greatest influence at that time.

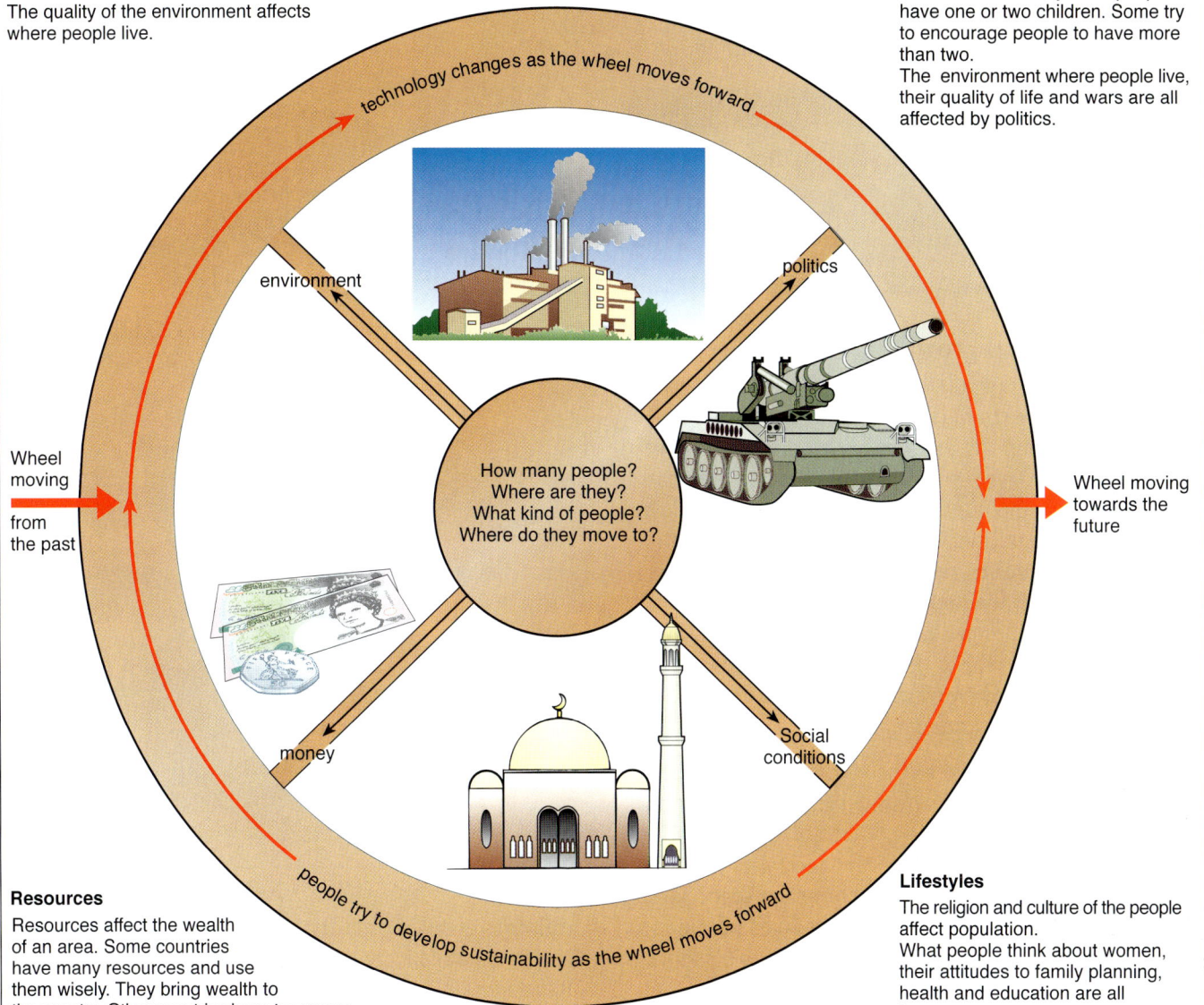

The Environment
How land used affects the environment.
The quality of the environment affects where people live.

Politics
Some countries only allow people to have one or two children. Some try to encourage people to have more than two.
The environment where people live, their quality of life and wars are all affected by politics.

technology changes as the wheel moves forward

environment

politics

Wheel moving

from the past

How many people?
Where are they?
What kind of people?
Where do they move to?

Wheel moving towards the future

money

Social conditions

people try to develop sustainability as the wheel moves forward

Resources
Resources affect the wealth of an area. Some countries have many resources and use them wisely. They bring wealth to the country. Other countries have too many people for their resources, and may be in debt and need aid.

Lifestyles
The religion and culture of the people affect population.
What people think about women, their attitudes to family planning, health and education are all important.
Working, literate women tend to have fewer children.

A

QUESTIONS

1 On an outline map of the world mark areas of low population density. Use different shadings or labels to show where conditions are too cold, too dry, too wet, too high or too steep for many people to live there.

2 Choose one of the places which is difficult to live in. Describe in more detail why it is difficult to live in that place.

3 Use the population wheel to explain other reasons for differences in population density.

SUMMARY

- Areas of low population density are in hostile environments.
- Not many people live there because survival is difficult.

FIND OUT MORE ▶ Ecosystems: 58 ▶ Frozen assets: 92

Policies from the cradle to the grave

FOCUS

- How quickly is the world's population growing?
- Is this growth the same in different parts of the world?

World population growth

In 1999 the world's population reached 6 billion. It will continue to grow even higher as long as the birth rate remains higher than the death rate. The birth rate is the annual number of live births per 1,000 people each year. The death rate is the number of deaths per 1,000 people each year. If you subtract the birth rate from the death rate, it will give you the rate of natural increase. This is the speed at which the population is growing. The world birth rate is 24 babies per 1,000 people and the death rate is 15 per 1,000. This gives us a natural increase of 24 – 15 = 9. This is often changed to a percentage. This becomes a 0.9 per cent annual increase.

High birth rates are linked to the world's fertility rate. The fertility rate is the average number of children born per woman. The world has a high fertility rate of 3. In some countries there is a high infant mortality rate. This means that for every 1,000 babies born each year a large number die in their first year. This encourages people to have more children, so that they know some will survive.

Death rates affect growth too. World life expectancy is 64 for males and 68 for females. This is linked to health care improvements.

World population increase is beginning to slow down. In the 1960s the rate of increase was 2 per cent per year which meant it had a doubling rate of 35 years. Generally as countries get richer their growth rates drop. Rich countries have an average fertility rate of 1.6 and poor

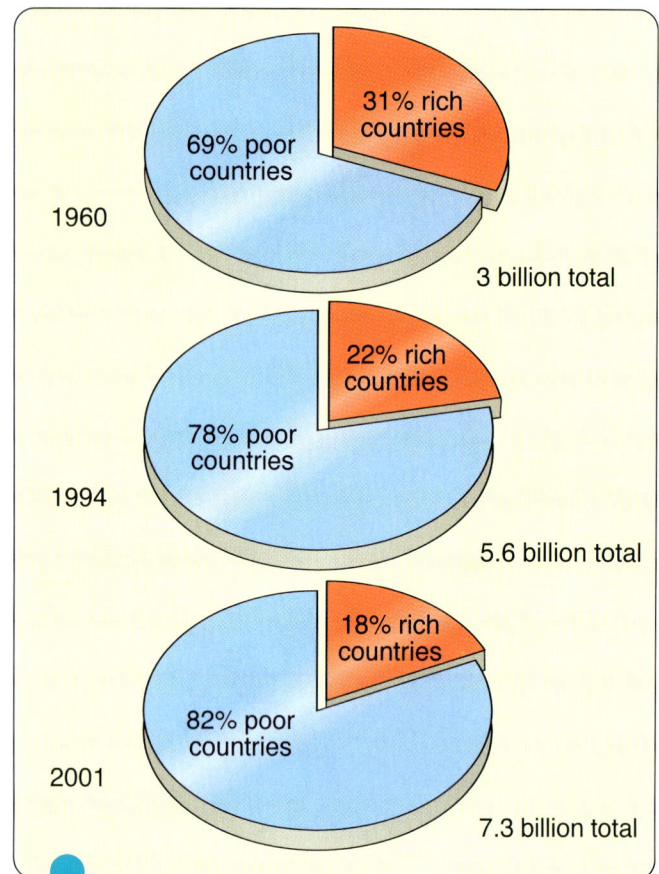

A Percentage of people living in rich and poor countries

countries an average of 3.4. Links between fertility rates and levels of education show that literate women in Bangladesh have fertility rates of 3 while illiterate women have rates of 5. The world's uneven population growth means that the proportion living in rich countries is being reduced.

Population policies

In some rich countries the governments are worried by low population growth rates. This could affect the success of the country since young people are a country's future.

CONTINENT	GNP US$	NUMBER OF COUNTRIES		
		Population is too high	Population is stable	Population is too low
Europe	12890	1	24	15
Asia	2360	19	21	6
Oceania	14370	6	3	0
Africa	630	41	11	1
N America	26210	0	2	0
S America	3310	18	14	1

B

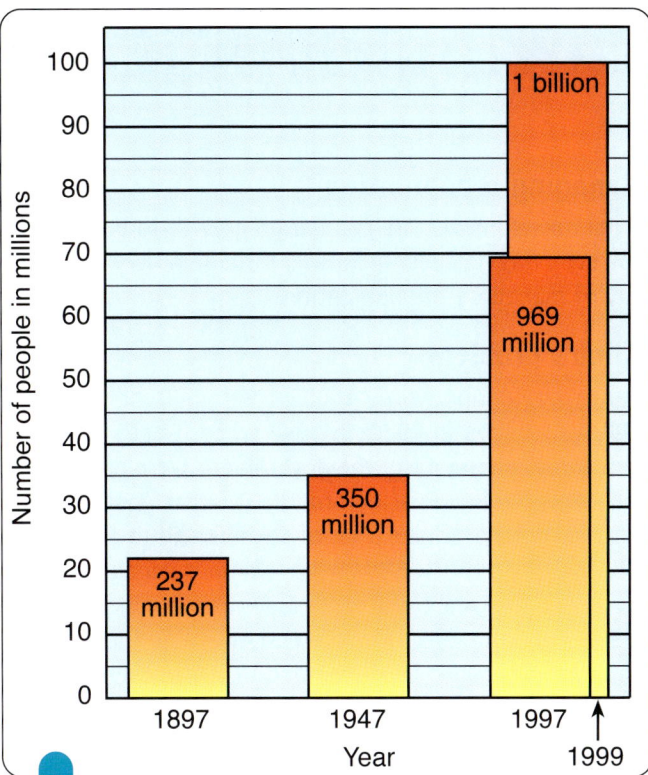

C Population growth in India

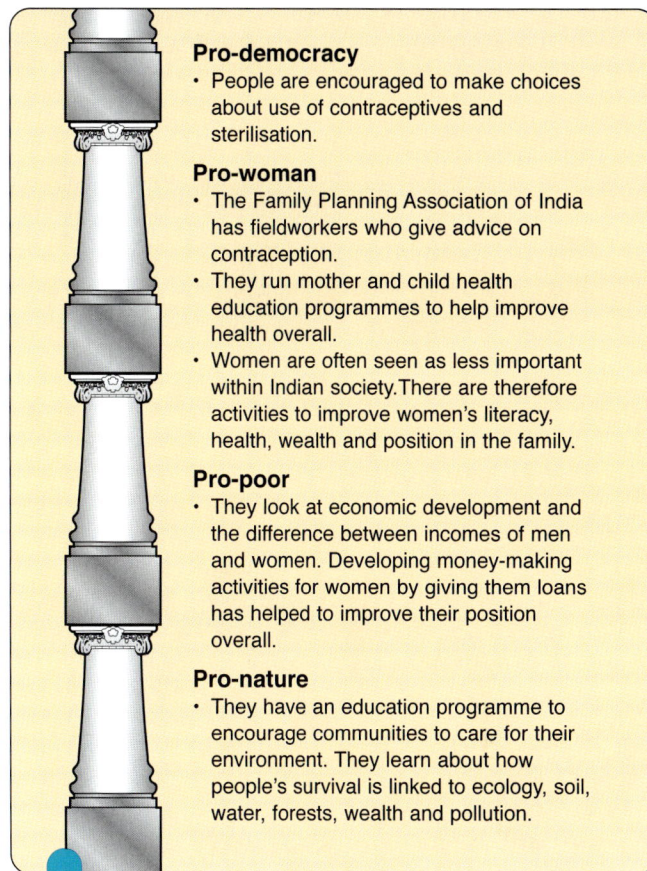

Chart showing Population growth in India. Y-axis: Number of people in millions (0 to 100). X-axis: Year.
- 1897: 237 million
- 1947: 350 million
- 1997: 969 million
- 1999: 1 billion

QUESTIONS

1 Draw your own family tree from the time of your grandparents' birth to today.
   a What is the fertility rate for each woman in your family?
   b Has this fertility rate increased or decreased with each generation?
   c Explain any differences between the generations.

2 In Bangladesh, women who can read and write tend to have fewer children than woman who are illiterate. Why do you think this is?

3 a Which continents have the greatest concerns about increasing populations?
   b How could they reduce their rate of population increase?

4 a Which continents are most worried about too few people?
   b How could they increase the rate of population increase?

5 What is the link between GNP and population growth rates shown in table **B**?

6 How could the world slow down its overall population growth rate?

D India's four pillars of population management

Pro-democracy
- People are encouraged to make choices about use of contraceptives and sterilisation.

Pro-woman
- The Family Planning Association of India has fieldworkers who give advice on contraception.
- They run mother and child health education programmes to help improve health overall.
- Women are often seen as less important within Indian society. There are therefore activities to improve women's literacy, health, wealth and position in the family.

Pro-poor
- They look at economic development and the difference between incomes of men and women. Developing money-making activities for women by giving them loans has helped to improve their position overall.

Pro-nature
- They have an education programme to encourage communities to care for their environment. They learn about how people's survival is linked to ecology, soil, water, forests, wealth and pollution.

In France the government encourages larger families by giving generous family allowances and bonus payments of 10,000 francs (over £1,300) per child. The government provides pre-school childcare and encourages mothers to combine a family and career.

India is likely to become the world's most populated country. Estimates are that India will overtake China by 2040.

Since 1951 India's governments have had policies to limit the birth rate. Family size has fallen and the number of couples using modern contraceptives has increased.

Improving the way of life of Indian people, and particularly women, can reduce population size. Population issues follow 'the four pillars' and are pro-democracy, pro-woman, pro-poor and pro-nature.

SUMMARY
- The world population is growing, although this has slowed down as some countries have become richer and more literate.
- The growth is greatest in the poor countries and slowest in the rich countries.

FIND OUT MORE ▷ Managing a population: 100 ▷ Lifstyle for growth: 100 ▷ Agenda 21: 108

China's plan for a growing population

FOCUS

- Why are there too many people in China?
- What has been done to help?

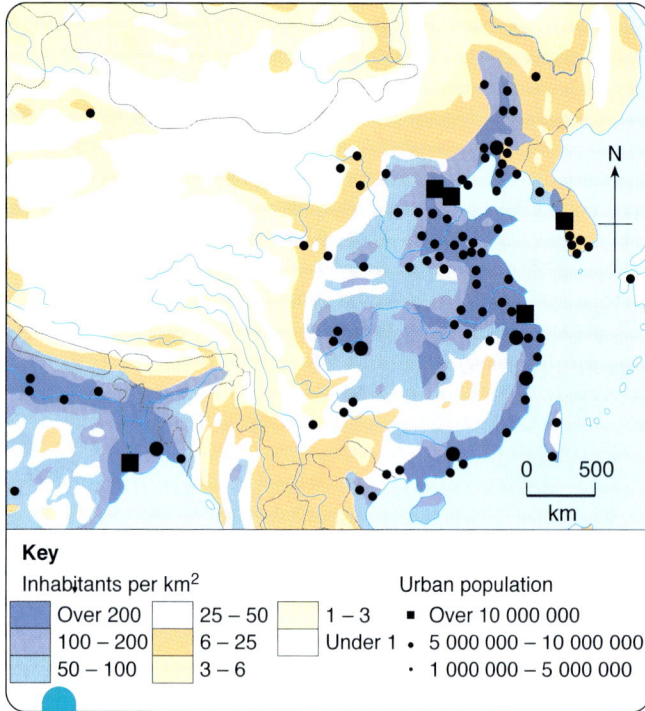

Key

Inhabitants per km²

Over 200	25 – 50
100 – 200	6 – 25
50 – 100	3 – 6
	1 – 3
	Under 1

Urban population
- Over 10 000 000
- 5 000 000 – 10 000 000
- 1 000 000 – 5 000 000

A Population, distribution and density in China

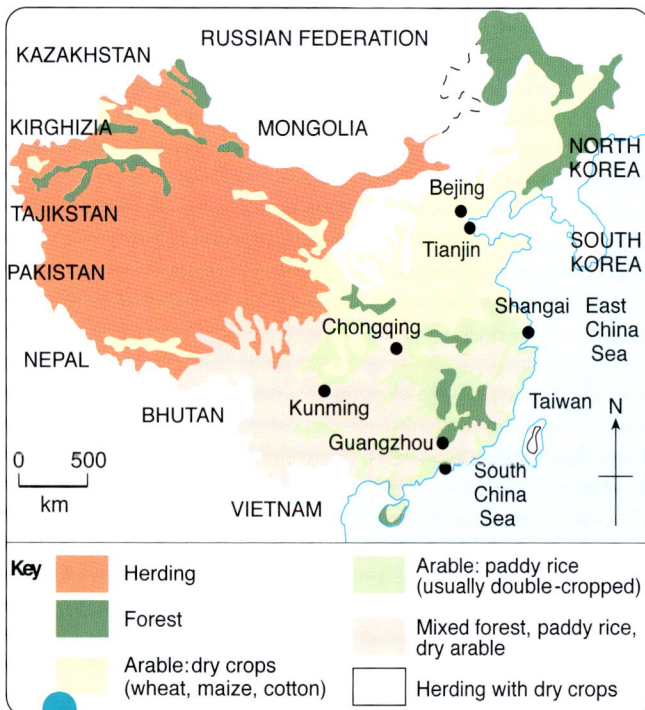

Key

- Herding
- Forest
- Arable: dry crops (wheat, maize, cotton)
- Arable: paddy rice (usually double-cropped)
- Mixed forest, paddy rice, dry arable
- Herding with dry crops

B Agricultural land use of China

Managing a population

China now considers its population growth to be stable. However, this has been achieved through a very unusual way of managing the population.

China's problem

China's population nearly doubled from 540 million in 1949 to 1 billion in 1980. In 1949 when it became ruled by the communist party the government were not worried about stopping population growth. It was a good thing for the country to have a lot of soldiers and to appear very strong. In the 1960s the government encouraged people to have more children. However a famine in the 1950s and early 1960s was an early warning that too many people meant too little food to share. There was simply not enough suitable land to grow food for all of the people. During the 1970s the Chinese government encouraged the use of contraceptives as it began a two-child policy. This meant couples were only allowed two children. It also encouraged later marriage and wider spacing between the children to delay the time the next generation were ready to marry. This was followed in 1980 by a one-child policy.

The one-child policy

Chinese people enjoyed increased benefits from the state in the 1980s but free education, priority housing, pensions and family benefit were taken away if a couple had a second child. The legal minimum age for marriage was set for 20 for women and 22 for men. People had to apply to the government for permission to get married and to have a child. This had to be changed slightly in 1984, when two children were eventually allowed for people living in rural areas if the first child was a girl. In the countryside, peasants had children for their future

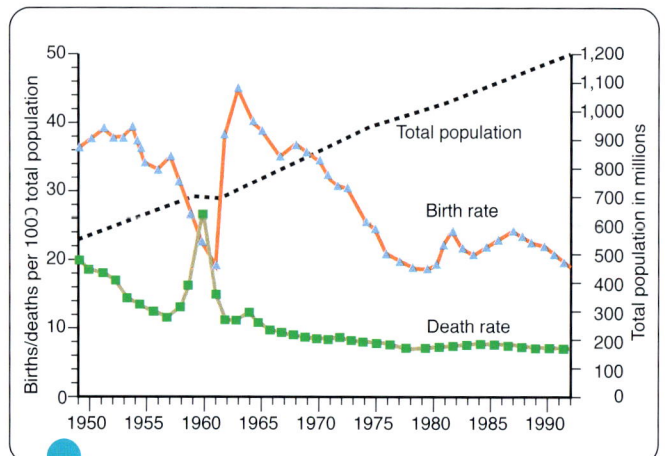

C Population change in China

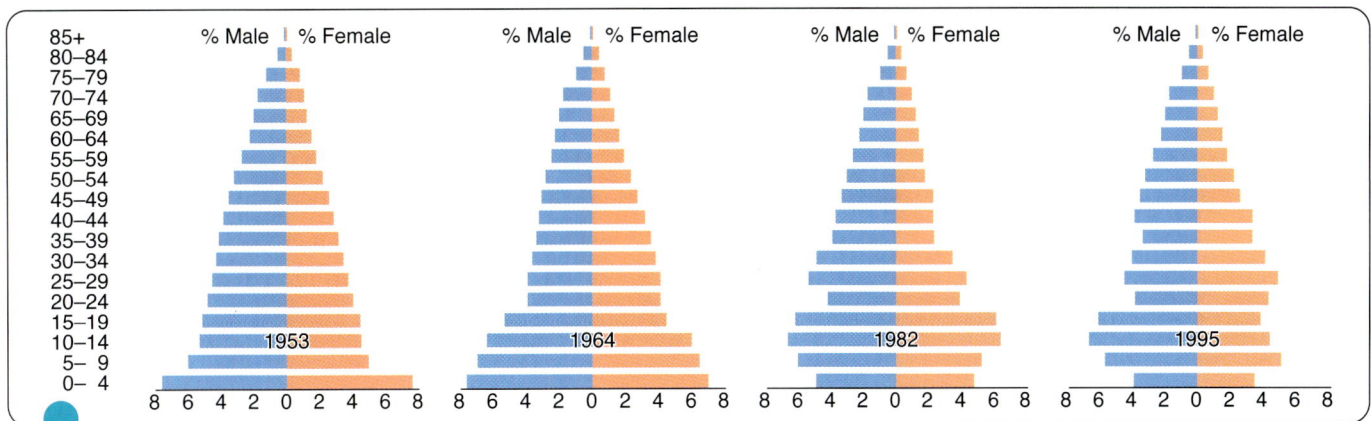

	% Male ‖ % Female	% Male ‖ % Female	% Male ‖ % Female	% Male ‖ % Female

Age groups (top to bottom): 85+, 80–84, 75–79, 70–74, 65–69, 60–64, 55–59, 50–54, 45–49, 40–44, 35–39, 30–34, 25–29, 20–24, 15–19, 10–14, 5– 9, 0– 4

Years: 1953, 1964, 1982, 1995

Axis scale: 8 6 4 2 0 2 4 6 8

D

wealth. Money is linked to sons rather than daughters. Daughters are expensive as they need a sum of money called a dowry when they marry. They then become part of their husband's family. Parents are then left with no one to support them in their old age. When only one child was allowed, some parents abandoned the girl babies after birth. There have also been cases of parents feeding poisonous berries to the girls or ending a pregnancy when they have found out through ultrasound scans that the child was a girl. This way they hoped that they would be able to try again for a boy.

In cities the one-child policy has been more successful. By 1995 the total fertility rate was reduced to 1.9 children per woman and 90 per cent used contraception. This was a major success in reducing the rapid rate of population growth. As the number of people being born is reduced, improved health care has also increased life expectancy. There are therefore more elderly people and the

population structure of the country is changing. The structure of the country shows how many people there are in each age group and of each different sex. We can tell what is happening by looking at population pyramids. Despite these measures, since 1980 a further 200 million people have been born in China and the population is unlikely to stabilise completely before 2030 when the population will be 1.5 billion. If China had not introduced this policy of having one child, the number of Chinese would be far higher than this.

SUMMARY

- China's resources were insufficient for the population growth it was experiencing.
- The one-child policy has stabilised the growth of population in China.

QUESTIONS

1 Look at maps **A** and **B**. Describe where most of China's people are found.

2 What effect did the famine of 1960s have on the birth and death rate of China? (graph **C**)

3 a What has happened to the number of young people under 15 since 1953? (graph **D**)
  b What has happened to the percentage of over 60s?
  c What has happened to the number of boys and girls?
  d Give reasons to explain these patterns.

4 Draw an outline of graph **C**. Make up a key; for example, if you think that Yan Chong and his brothers were likely to have died in 1979 then write letter c on your graph near 1979.

a Yan Chong and his brother Ye have been given injections against infectious diseases.

b Yan Chong now has three younger brothers.

c Yan Chong and his brothers die in a famine.

d There is plenty of food and Mr Chong and his wife decide to try and have more children.

e Mr Chong now has two more sons and a daughter.

f Mr Chong's brother and his wife can only have one child, the state have said that there is a one-child policy. They have a daughter.

g Mr Chong's brother lived in the countryside and has been allowed to have another child. He and his wife have a son.

Explain why you placed the statements on the graph in the different places.

FIND OUT MORE ▶ Living on the edge: 96 ▶ World population growth: 98

The many faces of China

FOCUS

- What are the positive social impacts of China's one-child policy?
- What are the negative social impacts of China's one-child policy?

What problems are there following one-child policy?

In January 1996 a television documentary on Channel 4 *Return to the Dying Rooms* told the story of some of the state-run orphanages in China. A report by Human Rights Watch showed records from a large orphanage in Shanghai which showed that children, most of them girls, had been starved to death on purpose. Other children were tied to beds, strapped on to potty chairs or left to look after themselves.

This sad C4 documentary started a lot of concern throughout the world. One couple decided to do something about this by adopting one of the children.

Not enough women

Today in China there are 52 million men in their early 20s who will never have a female partner. Remember that the population of the UK is 59 million!

Little emperors

China has 65 million only children. The generation of only children has been described as well developed intellectually, well fed and high achievers at school. This is due to the attention given to them. Sometimes they are referred to as 'little emperors'. They often find it difficult to get on with other people. Some cannot do simple things like tie shoelaces for themselves because other people have done everything for them.

Couple fly to China to adopt baby

A local couple made the 27 hour flight to the Southern City of Nanjing near Shanghai in June 1998 to bring home the little girl they had waited two years for and whom they had only ever seen in a photo.

'We found it quite hard to ignore the questions that were being raised in our minds,' they recalled. 'If there were already so many children that needed love, could we justify bringing another child into the world? Many Chinese girls are abandoned or given up for adoption because China, which already has a population of more than a billion, has a one-child policy and boys are the preferred sex.'

The couple decided to try inter-country adoption, going for China because British adoption regulations are accepted as legal in China.

In May of this year they received their first picture of the girl.

They were told that her natural parents had abandoned her on the steps of a green grocers in the city of Nanjing. 'Her parents left her in a public place because they knew she would be found and placed in an orphanage,' they said, 'but they took a huge risk because there is quite a hefty fine for abandoning a child. We were very impressed with the set up at the orphanage,' she continued. 'We met one of the carers who was in tears when she handed the child to us. All of the children were clean, well fed and looked happy and content.'

A

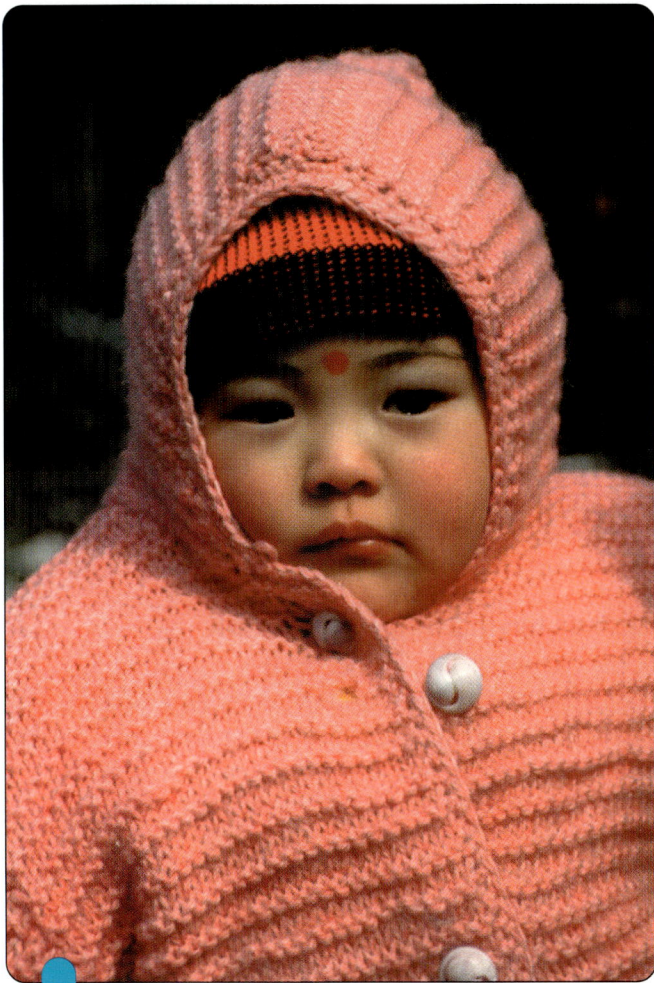

B Every year another 10% of the nation's urban children are classified as obese

'Would you have liked a brother or sister?'

'No, I think he or she may share everything – my clothes and other things.'

'Might it not have been good to share?'

'I don't think so. I have lots of beautiful things. When I go to the street, my mother may buy some drink for me, but if I have a sister she would buy one more and that would cost a lot.'

'Can you think of any problems with being the only child?'

'My parents hope I will achieve a lot, so I have to work hard to meet it. I am the only child, the only hope in the family.'

Indeed, many young couples will find themselves with eight grandparents to support by 2025 and there will be a quarter of the population over the age of 60.

QUESTIONS

1 What are the advantages and disadvantages of:
   a being a boy in China?
   b being a girl in China?

2 If you were an only child in China, what would be the good and bad parts of your life?

3 Use all the information on these pages to describe whether you think that the one-child policy has been a success. Give your reasons.

SUMMARY

- The one-child policy has led to a well-fed population which is not growing so fast.
- It has created an unnatural imbalance between ages and sexes within the population.

FIND OUT MORE ▶ World population growth: 98

Lifestyles for growth

FOCUS

- Why does population grow faster in poorer countries?
- How does the wealth of a country affect population growth?

Slowing population growth

In 1994 in Cairo there was a major conference for governments on population and development. The action plan it produced aimed to slow the world's population growth, so that the current population of 6 billion might stabilise at around 7.2 billion by 2050, rather than the 12.5 billion it could otherwise become.

Since 1968 the United Nations has stated that it has been a right for couples 'freely and responsibly to decide on the number and spacing of their children and to have information, education and the means to do so'. The International Conference on Population and Development in Cairo in 1994 reinforced this right by agreeing a plan which gives people the opportunity to plan their family size by making women as important as men, educating women and providing health schemes linked to giving birth.

Young workers

In Mali there is an average of 6.7 children in every family. These children help the family to survive. In rural areas they help with the farming. Childhood does not last long. Those in rural areas work at an earlier age than those in towns. By 10 to 12 years of age most children are helping their families. They are crucial to the economy and society. Unpaid work includes child minding, helping with household chores, farming, serving in shops, small trade, home industries, street selling, errand going, feeding animals, fetching water. This is very different to the way we think of children.

Cost of having a baby in the UK

In the UK the fertility rate is 1.7. This means that our population of 59 million is likely to decrease by 2025 to 57.2 million. We do not see children as a resource for our future in the same way as the children of Mali. People often wait to have children when they think they can afford to do so. Table C shows how expensive having children is in this country. Some people also plan for the financial future of their children.

POPULATION CHARACTERISTIC	UK (A RICH COUNTRY)	MALI (A POOR COUNTRY)
Birth rate per 1000	13	50
Death rate per 1000	11	20
Natural increase (percentage)	0.2	3
Doubling time	433 years	23 years
Population in 1999	59 million	23.7 million
Infant mortality per 1000	6.2	134
Fertility children per woman	1.7	6.7
Life expectancy male/female	74/79	44/48
Percentage urban	90	26
Percentage using contraception	72	7
Percentage female literacy	98	23

A Differences between the UK and Mali

B Childhood does not last long in Mali

Books and magazines £42
Maternity clothes £150
Nappies £650
Toys £350
Baby-sitting £954

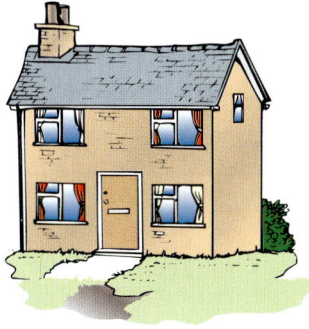

Clothes (birth to 5)
£934–£2,276
Food (birth to 5) £2,090
Food (birth to 16) £10,764
Christmas and birthdays
(birth to 5) £195–£1,820
Christmas
(5–16) £ up to £4,515
Cost at primary school £2,667
Cost at secondary school
£2,669

Pocket money (5–7) £1.09
a week
Pocket money (13–16) £4.04
a week
Pets £1,981
Holidays (birth to 21) £7,964
Transport (16–21) £3,289

Increased mortgage and
moving from a small
house to a three-bedroom
detached £10,000

C Counting the cost of our children's future

QUESTIONS

1 Put two headings, 'Mali' and 'UK'. Choose which of the following statements should go under each heading. Write out the two lists.
 • children are expensive
 • children work from an early age
 • many children
 • few children
 • many die young
 • many survive
 • can expect to live until 74
 • can expect to live to 44.

2 Use the figures from table **A** to answer the following questions:
 a Why will it be difficult to educate women in Mali?
 b Why is it difficult for women in Mali to reduce the number of children they have?

3 Do you think India's 4 pillars of population or China's one-child policy could be the best ways to tackle the increasing population problem in Mali? Give reasons for your choice.

How many children?

There are also differences in the ability to choose the number of children. In Mali the number of people using contraceptives is very low compared with the UK. The birth rate is very high but so is the infant mortality rate. If infant mortality rates are reduced, it has been shown that birth rates may eventually go down. This is because women believe their children will survive and therefore have fewer children. It is also clear that if you provide more education, then fertility rates change. The greater the level of education the lower the fertility rate in poor countries.

In some communities family size is determined by social customs and religious beliefs. In some societies such as Roman Catholic communities contraception and abortion is forbidden.

SUMMARY

• Today population grows faster in poor countries because of lower use of contraceptives, higher infant mortality, poverty and the traditions of larger families.
• Poorer countries have higher rates of population growth because they rely on large families for income and survival.

FIND OUT MORE ▷ World population growth: 98

LIVERPOOL HOPE UNIVERSITY COLLEGE

Grey Britain?

FOCUS

- **What is happening to the population structure in Britain?**
- **What is the impact of changes in the structure?**
- **What might the solutions be?**

The baby boomers

These people have one thing in common: they are both baby boomers. Many of your parents may fit into this category too! More than a million babies were born in the UK in 1964. This was the highest number born in one year since 1947, which was the record year. The baby boomers include all those born in the years 1961–71.

Baby boomer facts

- In 1991 there were fewer than 30 people of pensionable age for every 100 of working age.
- In 2023, when the 1960s baby boomers will be starting to reach their sixties, the ratio of those over 65 will double to 60 for every 100 people of working age.
- By 2025 there will be a million and a half more people aged 60–64 than in 1995.
- By 2021 the number of people over retirement age will be 17 million.
- Once in retirement more people will survive longer. Men can expect to live 21 years after retirement and women 25 years.

If your parents are in their thirties now, then they will be part of this large group of old people. Things have changed for these baby boomers as they near retirement age. Baby boomer men may have shorter working lives and may face lower pensions because of changes in the way people work. Many men no longer have a job for life, they change their employer more often, are often faced with unemployment or redundancy and may take time off to help to raise children. Baby boomer women may have greater pensions than women of previous generations, because more of them work.

As the baby boomers start to reach very old age in increasing numbers, health and social security services may not be able to help all of them. There may be more rationing of the NHS and social care for older people because it will be very expensive to look after everyone. There will be a shortage of younger relatives to act as carers as well as taxpayers to pick up the bill for welfare services. This is because fewer young people have been born since the baby boom.

The number of 'grey' voters who are over 65 will increase to 34 per cent in 2021, up from 24 per cent in 1997. These old people will have more voting power and no government will be able to ignore them. In the United States they are called the Grey Panthers and no president would dream of upsetting these important voters.

Frank Dobson, the Health Minister in 1999, said, 'As people approach old age many become anxious about how they will meet the cost of care. They are often unsure about how they will be looked after, who will pay and how much it will cost.'

A

B Problems for Britain in 2025

Councillor White, who is the first person to be responsible for elderly people in Coventry says, 'We won't cope unless there is a change in attitude. The problem is that many employers write people off in a job as they get older.' He says there are now four ages of man. Dependent

childhood, the working life, active retirement and dependent old age. 'Our aim is to extend that age of active retirement as much as we can through good eating, better exercise and preventative health.'

So what can be done to solve the problems of an ageing population? These are a few possible solutions:

- Encourage people to plan for their retirement.
- Provide support for those on low incomes.
- Encourage preventative health.
- Provide more services for old people.

QUESTIONS

1 How many people in the UK will be over retirement age in 2021?

2 If the population of the UK is now 59 million, what percentage of the population will this be?

3 What problems will the baby boomers cause Britain as they approach old age?

4 a Why are both the very young and the very old called 'dependent'?
  b How are these two groups dependent in different ways?

SUMMARY

- By 2031 Britain will have more people over the age of sixty.
- The cost of looking after an increasing number of elderly people will create problems for everybody.
- The solution is to plan for this problem now.

FIND OUT MORE ▶ **World population growth: 98**

An agenda for the 21st century

FOCUS

- What is Agenda 21?
- What can we do as part of our own agenda?

From Rio to Rotherham

In 1992 all the world's nations met at Rio de Janeiro to discuss the future of the planet. They agreed that the world's environmental problems could not be solved just by saving ecosystems. Environmental issues are issues linked to the problems and ambitions of people.

The Rio Conference produced Agenda 21– *A Document for the 21st Century*. Every country that signed up to the agreement was to think globally but act locally. Every local authority in each country was encouraged to develop its own Agenda 21. Small actions by each global citizen would be enough to make a difference. This would help everyone move towards sustainable development where the world would be left unharmed for future generations.

Agenda 21 says that communities should make decisions about their environment. Many communities throughout the world cannot make decisions to protect their environment until they have their own basic needs for survival. In Indonesia we know that it will be difficult to save the forests without helping the people financially.

If people become richer and literate, they often have smaller families. Smaller families may use fewer resources but only if countries act sustainably. There are many areas of our own lives where we can take responsibility and become better global citizens. Consider these facts before you think about your actions.

Transport

In the UK road transport creates 24 per cent of carbon dioxide emissions, 80 per cent of carbon monoxide and 40 per cent of nitrous oxides. These gases affect air quality and make breathing difficult for asthma sufferers. They also contribute to the greenhouse gases which cause global warming.

Waste

Most waste produced in the UK is sent to landfill sites. Every 18 months there is enough waste put in landfill sites in this country to fill Lake Windermere. Methane, which is a greenhouse gas, is produced as this rubbish decomposes.

Water

In the UK people use an average of 147 litres per person per day. Only 1 per cent of the treated drinking water is drunk. The rest goes down toilets or drains. Although Britain has a wet climate, the trend over recent years has been for less rainfall. When reservoirs empty we have to find more from underground supplies, which lowers the water levels in rivers and wetlands. This affects wildlife.

Energy

The UK produces about 2 per cent of the world's carbon dioxide. This is a gas which contributes to the greenhouse effect. Emissions of carbon dioxide can be reduced by encouraging renewable energy sources, such as wind power. In addition, about 20 per cent of energy used could be saved by energy conservation. Inefficient use of office machines alone costs business and schools up to £400 million a year.

Pollution

Pollution can take many forms – air, noise, water and land pollution – and is a risk to human health. Some pollution like acid rain can cross international borders.

Green purchasing

If the goods that people buy come from abroad, they use up more energy resources than those grown or made locally because more fuel is needed to transport them. Timber can be produced sustainably from a forest where careful management is carried out. Some goods such as coffee and cocoa can be produced so that they help the people who produce it, not just a few very rich people who buy and sell it. There are some difficult decisions to make when you weigh up whether or not we should buy fairly traded goods from countries far away. On one hand we are helping poor people, on the other hand we are causing more pollution because of the transport involved.

Transcport

- Use phone, email and other telecommunications systems where possible instead of paper-based ones which need transport
- Plan trips efficiently and car share wherever possible
- Use public transport or walk
- Encourage people not to leave their engines running on buses and cars when they come to pick up people from school

Waste

- Instead of throwing out surplus office materials or equipment, take them to a resource centre where things can be given to other people
- Encourage staff to re-use envelopes internally
- Use scrap paper to make your own note pads
- Only do the amount of photocopies that you really need, and double-side everything
- Use china mugs instead of plastic and paper cups
- Recycle any tin cans or glass bottles
- Encourage staff to recycle ink cartridges from photocopiers and printers

Water

- Put water saving devices in the cisterns of toilets. A simple plastic bottle filled with water in the toilet cistern will reduce the amount used
- Do not leave taps running
- Report leaks so that they can be mended

Energy

- Turn off the lights when you leave a room
- Switch off machines when they are not in use for more than 15 minutes. For computers, switch off the monitor when it is not being used
- Encourage staff to reduce the room temperature by 1°C. This will cut bills by 6–10 per cent
- Encourage staff to put in energy efficient lighting
- Encourage staff to insulate the building

Pollution

- Encourage staff to use cleaning materials which are environmentally friendly
- Encourage staff to avoid dangerous herbicides and pesticides in the school grounds
- Reduce use of vehicles around the school

A How could your school help?

QUESTIONS

1 a Write an Agenda 21 for your school. Write a list of what could be done by individuals in your school acting locally.
   b Explain how two of these actions will help the world.

2 Your headteacher may be worried about extra costs of acting environmentally. Write a letter to your headteacher explaining how these actions could be paid for.

3 a Write an Agenda 21 for your house.
   b Which of your actions do you think will be the most helpful for the world. Explain why.

SUMMARY

- Agenda 21 is a document that encourages people to act in a way that will look after the planet.
- We can all try to think globally and act locally.

FIND OUT MORE ▶ Reduce, re-cycle, re-use: 10 ▶ Forest conservation: 64–68
▶ The state of the environment: 86

Extensions

COUNTRY	POPULATION DENSITY PER KM^2
Brazil	1.96
Netherlands	47.64
Oman	1.12
Bahrain	86.24
Indonesia	11.6
Iceland	0.24

A

1 a Which of the countries in table **A** have low population densities?
  b Explain why they have low population densities.
  c Explain why Bahrain and the Netherlands have high population densities. Use an atlas to help you.

COUNTRY	BIRTH RATE PER 1000 PER YEAR	DEATH RATE PER 1000 PER YEAR	NATURAL INCREASE INCREASE	ANNUAL % INCREASE
Algeria	31	7		
Germany	10	11		
Mozambique	45	19		
Canada	13	7		
Italy	9	9		

B

2 a Copy table **B**.
  b Calculate the natural increase and percentage annual increase for each of the countries. Write your answers in the table.
  c Which of these countries might want to reduce their population growth rate? How might they solve this problem?
  d Which of these countries may want to increase their population growth rate? How might they solve this problem?

COUNTRY	GNP US $	FERTILITY RATE	INFANT MORTALITY
Niger	220	7.4	124
India	340	3.5	75
Germany	27510	1.3	5.1
UK	18700	1.7	6.2

C

3 a Look at table **C**. Write down the two poorest countries and the two richest.
  b Decide which of the statements below are true or false:
  • The lower the fertility rate, the richer the country.
  • The lower the fertility rate, the lower the infant mortality.
  • The higher the GNP, the lower the infant mortality.
  c Do you think that GNP or infant mortality has the greater effect on deciding how many children a woman has? Give reasons for your answer.

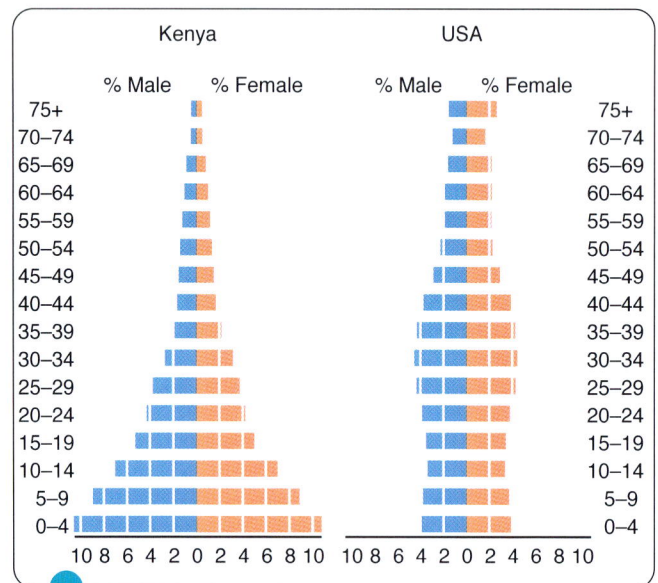

D

4 Look at graph **D**.
  a Describe the population structure of each of the two countries shown in the population pyramids.
  b Describe the problems that might be caused for each of these countries by their population structures.
  c What type of solutions could be offered to each of these countries?

Glossary

Acclimatise: People need to get used to differences in oxygen levels at different altitudes. Their body need to make more red cells to cope with reduced oxygen levels.

Agenda 21: A plan for the environment and the people of the world.

Birth rate: The number of live births per thousand of the population.

Death rate: The number of deaths per thousand of the population.

Densely populated: A large number of people per km^2.

Dependents: People such as young children and elderly people who need to be looked after by others.

Economic development: The change from being a poor country to becoming a richer country.

Family planning: Birth control used to plan the number and spacing of children.

Fertility rate: The number of children per woman.

GNP: Gross National Product – the total value of goods and services produced in a country. It is a measure of a country's wealth.

Infant mortality: The number of children per thousand who die before their first birthday.

Life expectancy: The average number of years a person is expected to live.

Natural increase: The difference between the birth and death rates.

Nomadic: Wandering without a fixed home.

Policies: Rules and statements that people follow.

Population density: The number of people per km^2.

Population Distribution: The way people are spread across an area – are they scattered or crowded together?

Rate of increase: The speed of natural increase in population.

Sparse population: Not many people per km^2.

United Nations: An international peace seeking organisation.

Index